PEOPLE OF THE OLD TESTAMENT

People of the Old Testament
FOR CHILDREN

Written by Gloria A. Truitt
Illustrated by Don Kueker

First Man on Earth

After God had made the earth,
  The heavens and the seas,
He turned the darkness into light
  And put forth plants and trees.
He made the birds, the fish, and beasts,
  According to His plan,
And then in His own image He
  Created the first man.
You'll find his name in Genesis—
  In case you didn't know—
Now, see if you can print it on
  The dotted line below.

Genesis 1:26-27; 3:17

___ ___ ___ ___

First Woman on Earth

Adam was a lonely man,
    So God made him a wife;
Because she was the first, she's called
    "The mother of all life."
Now, Cain and Abel were her sons,
    And so all generations
Began with this first woman who
    Gave birth to future nations.
Look up her name in Genesis,
    The Bible we believe,
And then you'll know what she was called;
    Her name was simply . . . !

Genesis 3:20

____ ___ ___

5

The Ark Builder

Once there was a godly man
    Who lived so long ago;
You can read about his life
    In Genesis, you know.
God said to him: "Now, build an ark.
    Then when it's done, go find
Each animal and bird; then bring
    A pair of every kind."
When they were safely in the ark,
    A flooding rain began
And lasted 40 days and nights,
    According to God's plan.
Now, when the rains had ended and
    The sun began to shine,

A dove was sent out from the ark,
    Which carried back a sign.
An olive branch proclaimed dry land,
    And so this family knew
That they could leave the ark quite soon
    With all the creatures, too.
They waited very patiently
    Until God spoke the Word:
"Go forth upon the earth and bring
    Each animal and bird."
Upon a mount called Ararat
    They offered thanks in prayer
To God, who saved them from the flood
    With His great, loving care.

I'm sure, by now, you've guessed the name
Of this old patriarch
Who listened to the Word of God
And built a mighty ark.

Genesis 7:15

___ ___ ___ ___

The Father of Believers

Four thousand years ago there lived
    A faithful patriarch.
Did you know he descended from
    The man who built the ark?
He herded cattle, sheep, and goats
    Owned by his father, Terah,
Then later on he took a wife;
    We know her name was Sarah.
God blessed them with an only son
    When they were very old.
Then with this child God tested him—
    In Genesis it's told.

God asked this man to sacrifice
    This dear, beloved son,
But then God stopped him just in time
    Before it could be done.
Who was this founding father of
    The faith we know today?
I'll give you one more little clue;
    His name begins with "A."

Genesis 22:10-13

—— —— —— —— —— —— ——

Jacob's Favorite Son

Jacob had a dozen sons,
    But one he favored more.
He gave this one a long-sleeved robe;
    Short sleeves the others wore.
His jealous brothers sold him down
    To Egypt as a slave,
But still, in spite of what they did,
    His brothers he forgave.
Their plot against this favored son
    Was mean and sinister,
But this young lad in time became
    The Pharaoh's minister!

He saved the land from famine
   By interpreting a dream,
And in the eyes of Pharaoh won
   Great honor and esteem.
He gave to all his relatives—
   His father Jacob, too—
The best of land in Goshen, where
   In peace their families grew.
Who was this son of Jacob whom
   All Israel proclaimed
To be their great and good protector?
   In Genesis he's named.

Genesis 47:5-6

— — — — — —

13

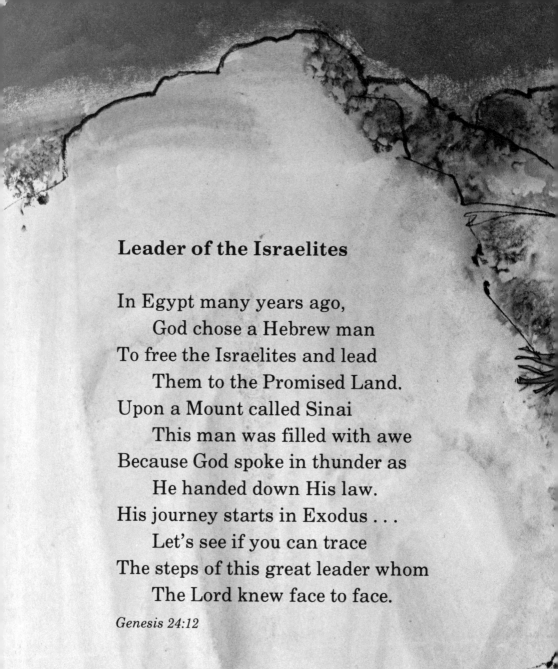

Leader of the Israelites

In Egypt many years ago,
    God chose a Hebrew man
To free the Israelites and lead
    Them to the Promised Land.
Upon a Mount called Sinai
    This man was filled with awe
Because God spoke in thunder as
    He handed down His law.
His journey starts in Exodus . . .
    Let's see if you can trace
The steps of this great leader whom
    The Lord knew face to face.

Genesis 24:12

___ ___ ___ ___ ___

Israel's Greatest Warrior

When Moses was quite old and frail,
    He chose another man
To lead the Israelites into
    The long-sought Promised Land.
They had to conquer Jericho—
    God told them what to do—
So, seven times they marched around
    The great, stone walls, then blew
Their trumpets. Then the walls fell down;
    This city now was theirs.
They celebrated joyously
    With victory songs and prayers.
Who was this greatest warrior,
    Who fought with just a sword,
And conquered the Land God promised them
    'Cause he listened to the Lord?

Joshua 6:1-7

—— —— —— —— ——

"Superman of the Old Testament"

Among God's people there was born
    A man who took great care
Not to lose his super strength
    By cutting his long hair.
He killed a lion with his hands
    And fought the Philistines,
Defeating them each time they tried
    To trap him with their schemes.
But once he told Delilah that
    His strength came from his hair,
She quickly snipped his "seven locks"
    While he was unaware.
The Philistines then captured him
    And took away his sight;
But then his hair grew back again,
    Along with his great might.

Now though he was a prisoner,
    And sadly could not see,
He toppled their great temple in
    A final victory.
Who was this mighty Israelite
    Whose strength earned him his fame?
Within the Book of Judges you
    Will surely find his name!

Judges 16:28-30

— — — — — — — — — —

A Loyal Daughter-in-Law

Once there was a widow who
    Showed love and loyalty
To her widowed mother-in-law
    Who met with poverty.

Now they had lived in Moab, but
    Her mother-in-law was from
The land of Judah, where they went—
    A trip quite wearisome.
A stranger to this land, she gleaned*
    The barley fields for food,
And through her dedication found
    Her happiness renewed.
Their story's in the Bible, and
    In it you'll find the truth . . .
Naomi was the mother-in-law;
    The daughter-in-law was . . . . !

Ruth 1:16

_____ _____ _____ _____

* The poor were allowed to gather stray stalks missed
by the reapers and keep all they found for their own use.
This was called "gleaning."

First King of Israel

When all the tribes of Israel
    Were split and quarreling,
They asked the prophet Samuel,
    "Would you appoint a king?"

A young and wealthy farmer was
    The king whom Samuel chose;
Then with his warriors he fought
    The Philistines, their foes.
He ruled for many years, then died
    Upon a battleground . . .
This mighty king of Israel
    Whom Samuel had found.
They say he was a handsome man,
    And stood so very tall.
Now see if you can guess his name;
    Of course, he was King . . . . !

1 Samuel 9:17

____ ____ ____ ____

Second King of Israel

A man called Jesse had eight sons;
  The youngest grew to fame
As a shepherd boy who had
    Uncommonly good aim.
He killed Goliath with a stone
    Slung from his shepherd's sling,
And when he grew to manhood, he
    Became a famous king.
He left to us the Book of Psalms . . .
    He sang to praise the Lord . . .
This second king of Israel,
    Whom everyone adored.
When he was very old, he died
    A rich and honored man.
Let's see if you can guess his name;
    By now I'm sure you can!

1 Samuel 17:48-50

____ ____ ____ ____ ____

Third King of Israel

The third king during the *golden age*
    Of Israel was wise,
And in Jerusalem He built
    A temple of vast size.
The country greatly prospered during
    His 40-year-long reign,
For culture, trade, and industry
    He managed to maintain.
Who was this son of David who
    Inherited the throne?
I'm sure that you can guess his name . . .
    He really is well-known!

1 Kings 11:42

___ ___ ___ ___ ___ ___

27

Who Was Swallowed by a Fish?

God sent a giant fish to save
    A frightened, drowning man . . .
This man was swallowed by the fish,
    According to God's plan.

Three days went by and then he was
    Spit out upon the beach,
So he could go to Nineveh
    To testify and preach.
Now, who was swallowed by the fish,
    But lived to teach God's way?
We find his story in the Bible;
    His name begins with "J."

Jonah 1:17

__ __ __ __ __

A Fearless Prophet

Long ago a man was cast
  Into a lion's den
By his enemies, who were
  A group of jealous men.
Because he had great faith in God,
  These animals he braved,
And by the power of the Lord,
  Surprisingly, was saved!
Who was this fearless prophet who
  Showed faith through bravery?
His book is in the Holy Bible;
  His name begins with "D."

Daniel 6:21-23

____ ____ ____ ____ ____ ____

Dear Parents,

Like us, God's people in the Old Testament were at the same time both sinners and saints. This book can help your child get acquainted with these ancient heroes of faith, who had far less of the light of God's revelation in Scripture to go by than we do.

"Whatever was written in former days was written for our instruction, that...we might have hope," the Bible says (Romans 15:4). It gives us hope when we read that, despite the failings of the men and women who are mentioned here, God never forsook His Old Testament people. He continued to show them kindess and finally climaxed His love for them and us by sending His dear Son Jesus to the cross to be the Savior of the world.

May you and your child have eternal salvation through faith in Him!

The Editor

Answers: First Man on Earth—Adam; First Woman on Earth—Eve; The Ark Builder—Noah; The Father of Believers—Abraham; Jacob's Favorite Son—Joseph; Leader of the Israelites—Moses; Israel's Greatest Warrior—Joshua; Superman of the Old Testament—Samson; A Loyal Daughter-in-Law—Ruth; First King of Israel—Saul; Second King of Israel—David; Third King of Israel—Solomon; Who Was Swallowed by a Fish?—Jonah; A Fearless Prophet—Daniel.